BEYOND
BLIND
BLAMING

BREAKTHROUGH JOURNAL

KEVIN D. ST.CLERGY

Beyond Blind Blaming
Breakthrough Journal
Copyright © 2025 by Kevin St.Clergy

For quantity and bulk order discounts, please email cc@blindblaming.com for more information.

ISBN (hardback): 979-8-9924942-1-1

Library of Congress Control Number:

Printed in the United States of America

CONTENTS

___

Introduction

THE POWER OF YOUR STORY

W HEN I WAS ELEVEN YEARS OLD, standing in the batter's box, watching strike after strike fly past me, I had no idea that my inability to hit the ball wasn't about effort, talent, or dedication. The year before, my batting average was .550, a number Babe Ruth would be proud of at the height of his career (.394). I was a rising star. A hero. In just one season, I went from hero to zero.

The parents blamed my attitude, my swing, my motivation, you name it. Then I started blaming myself. I felt like a complete failure. But it was about something much simpler—I couldn't see clearly. Nobody realized I needed glasses. Not my coaches, not my parents, and certainly not me.

This journal is about that moment of clarity that changes everything. The moment when you finally see what's been hiding in plain sight.

We all have stories where we've blamed the wrong things – ourselves, others, circumstances – only to discover later that the real issue was something entirely different. These stories aren't just interesting anecdotes; they reveal powerful patterns that shape our lives, relationships, and achievements.

Blind Blaming happens when we attribute our challenges to the wrong causes because we're missing crucial information. Like my baseball story, it often feels completely logical at the time. Everyone, including me, thought my problem was effort, attitude, or technique. No one considered my vision.

Your personal stories hold the key to identifying your own blind blaming patterns. As you journey through this journal, you'll uncover these patterns, challenge your assumptions, and discover breakthroughs hiding in plain sight.

HOW TO USE THIS JOURNAL

This journal is designed to be both a companion and catalyst for transformation. Each section builds on the previous one, guiding you through a process of discovery and change:

1. **Write honestly** – This is your private space for authentic reflection

2. **Embrace discomfort** – The most powerful insights often arise from challenging questions

3. **Return and review** – Revisit earlier entries as new insights emerge

4. **Connect the dots** – Look for patterns across different exercises

5. **Take action** – Use the commitment sections to move from insight to implementation

There's no "right way" to use this journal. You might work through it sequentially or skip to sections that resonate most. You might complete it in days or take months to process deeply. The journey is yours.

What matters most is your willingness to look beyond the obvious, to question your assumptions, and to discover what's really holding you back.

YOUR
COMMITMENT

I commit to approaching this journey with:

- Curiosity instead of certainty
- Openness to discovering my blind spots
- Willingness to consider alternative explanations
- Courage to act on what I discover

Signature: ....

Date: ....

Exercise

UNCOVERING YOUR BLIND BLAMING STORY

STORY DISCOVERY PROMPTS

Take a moment to reflect on a significant experience in your life where despite your best efforts, you couldn't make progress. Later, you discovered the real issue was something entirely different than what you initially thought. You might not have discovered what is really happening yet and that is ok. Just write down the story below.

If you're having trouble identifying a story, consider these prompts:

- A time when you kept trying harder but results got worse
- A recurring relationship pattern that suddenly made sense
- A health challenge that turned out to have an unexpected cause
- A professional obstacle that resolved once you saw it differently
- A situation where everyone (including you) misdiagnosed the problem

■ **Write your story below. Don't worry about perfect writing—focus on capturing the experience authentically.**

STORY ANALYSIS FRAMEWORK

Now, let's analyze your story to understand the blind blaming pattern:

■ **What did you believe was the problem?**

_____

_____

_____

_____

■ **Who or what did you blame?**

_____

_____

_____

_____

■ **How did this explanation make sense at the time?**

_____

_____

_____

_____

_____

■ **What evidence did you collect that supported your explanation?**

_____

_____

_____

■ **What was eventually revealed as the real issue?**

_____

_____

_____

■ **What made this real issue initially invisible to you?**

_____

_____

_____

■ **What changed that allowed you to see the truth?**

_____

_____

_____

THE BREAKTHROUGH MOMENT

■ **Describe the moment when you finally saw what was really happening:**

_____

_____

_____

_____

_____

_____

_____

■ **How did it feel to discover the real issue?**

_____

_____

_____

_____

■ **What became possible once you saw the truth?**

....

....

....

....

....

STORY SHARING GUIDE

Your blind blaming story is powerful—not just for your own growth but potentially for others. Consider how you might share this story to help someone else recognize their own patterns:

Key elements to include when sharing your story:

■ What you initially believed vs. what was actually happening
■ Why the explanation seemed logical at the time
■ The moment of clarity that changed everything
■ The transformation that followed

■ **What would be the most important takeaway for someone hearing your story?**

....

....

....

....

STILL SEARCHING?

If you're having trouble identifying a clear blind blaming story from your past, that's completely normal. Sometimes we're still in the middle of the story, and the breakthrough hasn't happened yet.

Here are some alternate approaches:

- **Current Situation Analysis:** Think about a current challenge where you feel stuck despite your best efforts. What explanations have you accepted? What might you be missing?

....

....

....

....

....

- **Observer Exercise:** Recall a situation where you watched someone else blame the wrong thing for their challenges. What could they see that they couldn't?

....

....

....

....

....

■ **Pattern Recognition:** List three recurring challenges in your life. For each one, ask: "What if my explanation is wrong? What else might be happening?"

As you progress through this journal, you'll develop greater clarity about your blind blaming patterns. You may discover that what you thought was your story changes as you gain new insights. That's not just normal—it's part of the transformation process.

Your breakthrough begins the moment you question what you've always believed to be true.

Turn the page to begin Section One: Awareness, where we'll explore the foundations of Blind Blaming and how to recognize it in your life.

01

SECTION ONE

AWARENESS

Chapter 1

UNDERSTANDING BLIND BLAMING

WE ALL HAVE BLIND SPOTS—AREAS where danger lurks beyond our vision. Blind blaming works the same way, shaping our decisions and derailing our progress while remaining conveniently out of sight. This chapter is about turning on the lights and seeing what's been hiding in plain sight.

BLIND BLAMING: THE ESSENTIALS

Definition: Blind Blaming is the unconscious pattern of attributing problems to the wrong causes because crucial information or insights are missing. It is "blind" because the real issue cannot be seen. It is "blaming" because we instinctively want to assign fault somewhere—even if it's to ourselves.

Three Fatal Flaws of Blind Blaming:

1. **Blind Blaming Feels Right**
   It feels completely logical based on the information we have.

2. **Blind Blaming Is Self-Reinforcing**
   Once we decide on a cause, we seek evidence confirming our belief.

3. **Blind Blaming Blocks Real Solutions**
   While focused on the wrong problem, we can't solve the right one.

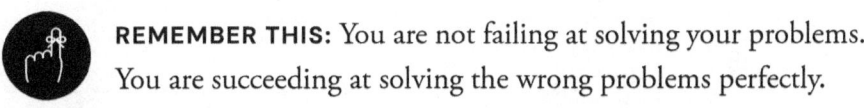 **REMEMBER THIS:** You are not failing at solving your problems. You are succeeding at solving the wrong problems perfectly.

CONNECTING TO YOUR STORY

Look back at the blind blaming story you shared in the introduction. How do you see the three fatal flaws playing out?

■ **How did your explanation feel completely logical at the time?**

....

....

....

....

■ **What evidence did you collect that reinforced your explanation?**

....

....

....

....

■ **How did focusing on the wrong problem block you from finding the real solution?**

....

....

....

....

THE PSYCHOLOGY BEHIND BLIND BLAMING

Our minds are wired with shortcuts that can lead us astray. Below are three cognitive biases that often fuel blind blaming. Check any that you recognize from your story:

- **Confirmation Bias:** Once we believe in something, we become treasure hunters obsessed with finding proof we are right. *How this showed up in my story:*

....

- **Self-Serving Bias:** We credit ourselves for wins but blame outside factors for losses. *How this showed up in my story:*

....

- **Availability Bias:** Our minds grab the first explanation within reach, like someone frantically searching a dark room but only looking where the flashlight beam lands. *How this showed up in my story:*

....

- **Which bias do you think most strongly affects your decision-making in general? Why?**

....

....

....

....

RECOGNIZING BLIND BLAMING IN YOUR LIFE

Below are five warning signs that blind blaming might be at work in your life right now. For each one, rate how strongly it applies to your current situation on a scale of 1-5 (1 = Not at all, 5 = Very strongly):

1. Recurring Problems: The same challenges keep reappearing despite various solutions.
Where I notice this in my life:

2. Escalating Frustration: You're working harder but seeing less progress.
Where I notice this in my life:

3. Relationship Strain: People around you seem defensive or communication breaks down.
Where I notice this in my life:

4. Diminishing Confidence: You question your abilities more frequently than you used to.
Where I notice this in my life:

5. Supportive Sabotage: Well-intentioned advice leaves you feeling worse, not better.
Where I notice this in my life:

TOTAL SCORE?

■ *What does this mean to you?*

....

....

....

....

■ **Looking at your ratings, which warning sign appears most strongly in your life right now?**

....

....

....

....

■ **What might this be telling you about where to focus your attention?**

....

....

....

....

YOUR BLIND BLAMING PATTERNS

Think about a current challenge where you feel stuck.

1. **Write** the challenge you're facing.
2. **List** what or who you currently blame.
3. **Note** the solutions you've tried based on these explanations.

■ What is your challenge?

....

....

....

....

■ What patterns do you notice?

....

....

....

....

■ What alternative explanations haven't you considered yet?

....

....

....

....

THE COST OF MISSING HIDDEN TRUTHS

When we miss the hidden truths in our lives, the costs cascade through every vital dimension. For your current challenge, consider:

■ **Impact on your health (energy, stress, physical well-being):**

....

....

....

■ **Impact on your wealth (time, money, resources):**

....

....

....

■ **Impact on your personal and work relationships (trust, connection, communication):**

....

....

....

■ **Total estimated cost (financial, emotional, opportunity):**

....

....

■ **What surprises you most about these costs?**

....

....

....

REFLECTION QUESTIONS _____

1. What was your most significant insight from this chapter?

....

....

....

2. Where else in your life might you be experiencing blind blaming?

....

....

....

3. What assumptions do you make that might be limiting your perspective?

_____

_____

_____

4. What would become possible if you discovered the real issue?

_____

_____

_____

COMMITMENT TO AWARENESS

Based on what you've discovered in this chapter, what is one specific action you can take this week to begin challenging your blind spots?

▪ **I commit to:**

_____

▪ **When I will do this:**

_____

▪ **How I will hold myself accountable:**

_____

▪ **How will I punish myself if I don't do this?**

_____

JOURNAL PROMPT: Before moving on to the next chapter, take a moment to write freely about what's emerging for you. What connections are you making? What questions are arising? What feels most important to explore further?

....

....

....

....

....

....

....

....

....

....

Breaking free from Blind Blaming begins with awareness. Simply recognizing these patterns creates the possibility for transformation. As you continue this journey, be gentle with yourself while remaining courageously honest about what you discover.

Turn the page to explore Chapter 2, where we'll learn how to move from Negativity to Possibility.

Chapter 2

NEGATIVITY TO POSSIBILITY

HE JOURNEY FROM STAGNATION to success begins with a fundamental shift in how we respond to challenges. When we release our grip on blame and complaints, we free up the mental and emotional energy needed to spot opportunities, solve problems, and create real change.

THE ACT FORMULA: YOUR PATHWAY TO POSSIBILITY

THE ACT FORMULA

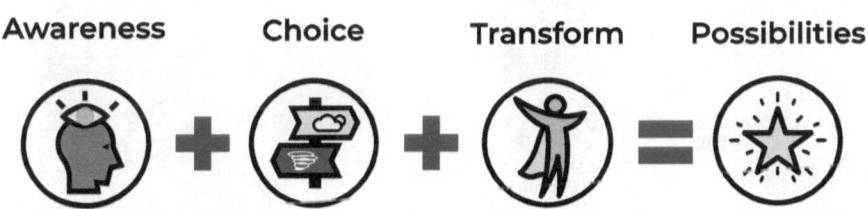

Awareness   Choice   Transform   Possibilities

Definition: The ACT Formula provides a systematic approach to move from negative patterns into possibilities:

Awareness + **C**hoice + Transform = **Possibilities**

This formula represents a practical pathway from reaction to action:

- **Awareness** of our thoughts and patterns
- Conscious **Choice** about our responses
- Actions that **Transform** our relationship to challenges
- Expanded **Possibilities** in our lives

REMEMBER THIS: This isn't about forcing positivity; it's about choosing productivity. When you catch yourself blaming or complaining, ask: "What problem am I actually trying to solve here?" And, "Is this the most effective way to solve it?"

CONNECTING TO YOUR STORY

Revisit your blind blaming story and identify where the ACT Formula could have created an earlier breakthrough:

- **Awareness:** What signals or patterns might you have noticed sooner?

....

....

....

- **Choice:** What different choice could you have made in response?

....

....

....

- **Transform:** How could that choice have transformed your approach?

....

....

....

- **Possibilities:** What might have become possible with this shift?

....

....

....

THE HIDDEN COST OF BLAMING AND COMPLAINING

Research shows that chronic complaining:

- Rewires neural pathways toward negativity
- Increases stress hormones
- Weakens immune function
- Strains relationships
- Blocks creative problem-solving

■ For one day, track your blame and complaint patterns in the log below:

Time	Situation	Blame/Complaint	Energy Level (1–10)	Impact on Others

■ **What patterns do you notice about when and why you blame or complain?**

....

....

....

....

■ **How do these patterns affect your energy and relationships?**

....

....

....

....

THE INSIGHT-IMPLEMENTATION MATRIX

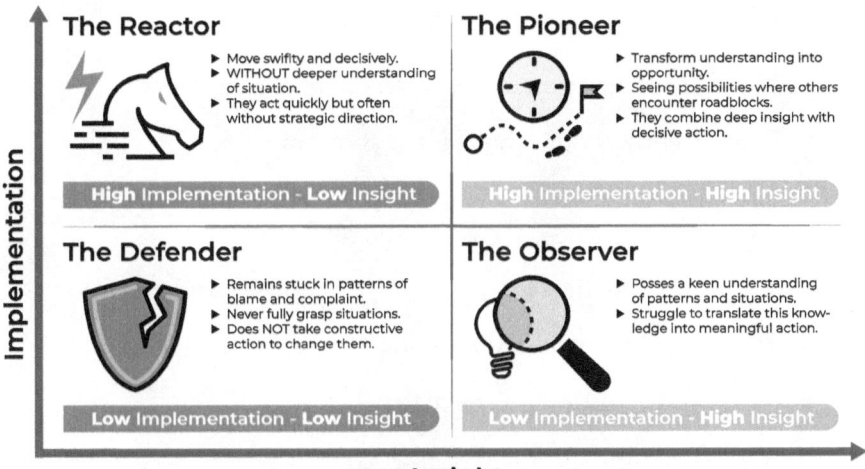

Implementation (vertical axis label)

The Reactor
- Move swiftly and decisively.
- WITHOUT deeper understanding of situation.
- They act quickly but often without strategic direction.

High Implementation - **Low** Insight

The Pioneer
- Transform understanding into opportunity.
- Seeing possibilities where others encounter roadblocks.
- They combine deep insight with decisive action.

High Implementation - **High** Insight

The Defender
- Remains stuck in patterns of blame and complaint.
- Never fully grasp situations.
- Does NOT take constructive action to change them.

Low Implementation - **Low** Insight

The Observer
- Posses a keen understanding of patterns and situations.
- Struggle to translate this knowledge into meaningful action.

Low Implementation - **High** Insight

Insight (horizontal axis label)

The Insight-Implementation Matrix reveals how you typically respond to challenges by mapping two critical capabilities:

- Your ability to recognize patterns of blame and complaint (insight)
- Your capacity to take constructive action (implementation)

For each statement below, rate yourself from 1–5 (1 = Rarely true, 5 = Almost always true):

Insight Dimension:

1. I quickly recognize when I'm blaming or complaining: ....

2. I can identify the underlying causes of my frustrations: ....

3. I notice patterns in how I respond to challenges: ....

4. I'm aware of how my reactions affect others: ....

5. I understand the difference between problems and symptoms: ....

Implementation Dimension:

1. I take prompt action on my insights: ....

2. I follow through on commitments to change: ....

3. I convert complaints into constructive solutions: ....

4. I implement new approaches when old ones aren't working: ....

5. I consistently act on what I learn about myself: ....

Plot Your Position:

- Total your Insight score: .... (horizontal axis)

- Total your Implementation score: .... (vertical axis)

- Circle your position on the matrix below:

THE INSIGHT-IMPLEMENTATION MATRIX

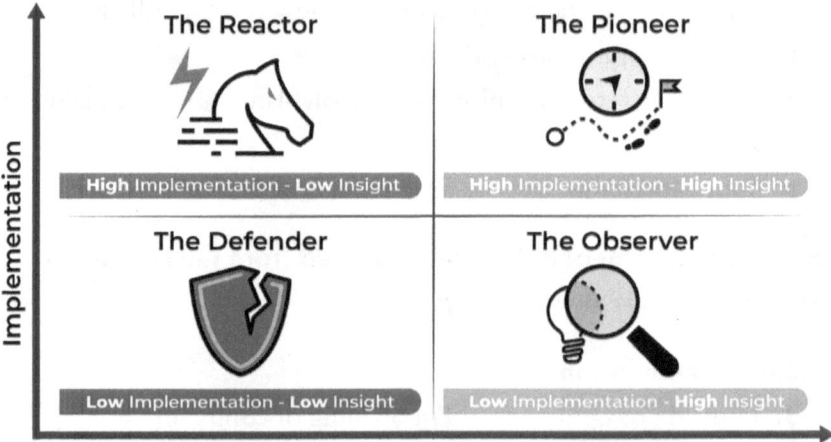

■ **What does your position reveal about your strengths and growth areas?**

....

....

....

....

■ **What one shift would help you move toward the Pioneer quadrant?**

....

....

....

....

PRACTICING THE ACT FORMULA

Let's apply the ACT Formula to a current challenge you're facing:

- **Identify a current situation where you find yourself blaming or complaining:**

....

....

....

....

....

AWARENESS:

- What patterns do you notice in your thoughts, feelings, or behaviors?

- What triggers your blame or complaints in this situation?

....

....

....

....

....

CHOICE:

- What is the Power Pause you could take when these patterns arise?

- What different perspective could you choose in that moment?

....

....

....

....

TRANSFORM:

- What specific action could transform your relationship to this challenge?

- How could you channel your energy toward solutions instead of blame?

....

....

....

....

POSSIBILITIES:

■ What becomes possible with this new approach?

■ How might others respond differently to this shift?

....

....

....

....

....

CULTIVATING THE POWER PAUSE

The space between stimulus and response is where your freedom lies. Practice these three Power Pause techniques this week:

1. **The Three-Breath Pause** When triggered to blame or complain, take three slow, deep breaths before responding.

2. **The Curiosity Question** Replace immediate judgment with: "What might I be missing here?"

3. **The Possibility Pivot** Ask yourself: "What opportunity might exist in this challenge?"

■ **Which of these Power Pause techniques feels most accessible to you right now? Why?**

....

....

....

....

■ **In what specific situations will you practice your chosen technique this week?**

....

....

....

....

REFLECTION QUESTIONS

1. How has blaming or complaining been serving you? What needs does it meet?

....

....

....

....

2. What shifts in energy do you notice when you move from blame to possibility?

....

....

....

....

....

3. Who in your life models the ability to focus on possibilities rather than problems?

....

....

....

....

....

4. What one situation would transform most significantly with a different focus?

....

....

....

....

....

COMMITMENT TO POSSIBILITY

Based on what you've discovered in this chapter, choose one specific blame pattern to transform this week:

■ **The blame pattern I commit to shifting is:**

....

■ **Instead of blaming or complaining, I will:**

....

■ **I will practice this shift in these situations:**

....

■ **I will know I'm successful when:**

....

JOURNAL PROMPT: Before moving on to the next chapter, reflect on what happens when you release blame and open to possibility. What feels uncomfortable about this shift? What feels liberating? What insights are emerging about your relationship to control and uncertainty?

....

....

....

....

Moving from negativity to possibility isn't about denying problems. It's about approaching them with energy that supports solutions rather than reinforces limitations. Each time you make this shift; you strengthen your capacity to create meaningful change.

Turn the page to explore Chapter 3, where we'll uncover the Blame Loop that keeps us stuck in recurring patterns.

Chapter 3

THE BLAME LOOP REVEALED

THE BLAME LOOP™ IS A PSYCHOLOGICAL roundabout where every exit seems to lead back to the entrance. This loop is not just a cycle of failure; it is a masterfully disguised trap that keeps us investing time, energy, and hope into solving the wrong problems.

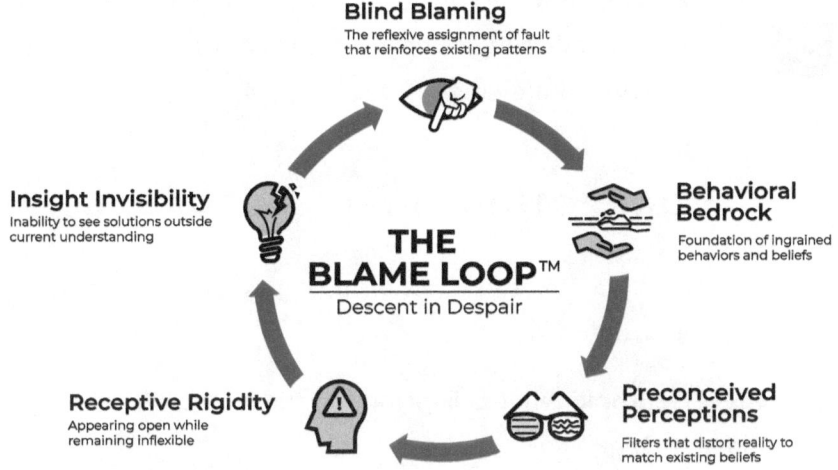

Blind Blaming
The reflexive assignment of fault that reinforces existing patterns

Behavioral Bedrock
Foundation of ingrained behaviors and beliefs

Preconceived Perceptions
Filters that distort reality to match existing beliefs

Receptive Rigidity
Appearing open while remaining inflexible

Insight Invisibility
Inability to see solutions outside current understanding

THE BLAME LOOP™
Descent in Despair

THE BLAME LOOP: UNDERSTANDING THE CYCLE

Definition: The Blame Loop is a self-reinforcing cycle where each component strengthens the others, creating a prison of perception that keeps you trapped solving the wrong problems.

The Five Components:

1. **Behavioral Bedrock:** The foundation of beliefs that shape how you see problems

2. **Preconceived Perceptions:** The filters that determine what information you accept or reject

3. **Receptive Rigidity:** The illusion of openness while remaining inflexible

4. **Insight Invisibility:** The inability to see solutions that don't fit your current paradigm

5. **Blind Blaming:** The keystone that holds the entire system in place

 **REMEMBER THIS:** Like removing a keystone can cause an arch to collapse, addressing Blind Blaming can bring down the entire structure of limitation.

CONNECTING TO YOUR STORY

Revisit your blind blaming story and identify how each component of the Blame Loop manifested:

■ **Behavioral Bedrock:** What beliefs formed the foundation of your misunderstanding?

Preconceived Perceptions: What information did you filter out that might have helped?

....
....
....
....

Receptive Rigidity: How did you appear open while actually remaining closed to alternatives?

....
....
....
....

Insight Invisibility: What solutions were invisible to you at the time?

....
....
....
....

- **Blind Blaming:** What or who did you blame that reinforced the entire cycle?

_____

_____

_____

_____

MAPPING YOUR CURRENT BLAME LOOP

Think about a current challenge where you feel stuck. For each component, identify how it might be operating:

- **Behavioral Bedrock:** What deep-seated beliefs might be shaping how you see this challenge?

_____

_____

_____

_____

- **Preconceived Perceptions:** What information might you be filtering out or dismissing?

_____

_____

_____

_____

■ **Receptive Rigidity:** Where might you be saying "I'm open to alternatives" while actually remaining fixed?

_____

_____

_____

_____

■ **Insight Invisibility:** What solutions might be invisible to you because they don't fit your current thinking?

_____

_____

_____

_____

■ **Blind Blaming:** What or who are you blaming that keeps this cycle in motion?

_____

_____

_____

_____

■ **Looking at this map, what pattern do you notice about how your Blame Loop operates?**

....

....

....

....

EXPLORING THE FIVE COMPONENTS

Let's dive deeper into each component to better understand how they work in your life:

1. Behavioral Bedrock: The Foundation of Failure

Your Behavioral Bedrock isn't just the foundation of your mental house; it's the ground beneath it. Like geological layers formed over time, it has been shaped by early experiences, cultural conditioning, past successes, and deep-seated beliefs.

■ **What early experiences have shaped how you approach challenges?**

....

....

....

- What beliefs about "how things should work" might be limiting your perspective?

....

....

....

....

2. Preconceived Perceptions: The Filters That Fail Us

Our perceptual filters are like sophisticated distortion machines that process reality into what we're willing to see while filtering out anything that challenges our existing beliefs.

- What evidence have you recently dismissed because it didn't fit your expectations?

....

....

....

....

- What might you be overlooking in your current challenge?

....

....

....

....

3. Receptive Rigidity: The Prison We Praise

The most cunning aspect of this prison is that the stronger its walls become, the more we praise our openness. We become so convinced of our receptivity that we can't see our rigidity.

■ **Where do you pride yourself on being open-minded while actually remaining fixed?**

....

....

....

....

....

■ **How might your "openness" actually be protecting you from uncomfortable truths?**

....

....

....

....

....

4. Insight Invisibility: The Blindness We Can't See

Our brains are wired to see what we expect to see and to make anything that doesn't fit vanish from awareness. It's not that we actively reject solutions. They simply don't register in our consciousness.

What solutions might be hiding in plain sight in your current situation?

_____

_____

_____

_____

_____

Who might see possibilities that are currently invisible to you? Coaches, Mastermind Group Members, or?

_____

_____

_____

_____

_____

5. Blind Blaming: The Keystone of Chaos

Blind Blaming is the keystone that holds the entire psychological arch in place, reinforcing each component we've discussed.

■ **What forms of sophisticated blame do you engage in?**

....

....

....

....

....

■ **How does your blame pattern protect you from facing deeper truths?**

....

....

....

....

....

....

THE VICIOUS CYCLE:
WHY IT'S SO HARD TO BREAK FREE

The more times we cycle through the Blame Loop, the more it becomes like psychological, unbreakable bedrock—layers of beliefs compressed over time until they seem as solid as stone.

■ **Draw your personal Blame Loop cycle below, showing how one component leads to the next:**

■ **What keeps this cycle spinning in your life?**

....

....

....

....

■ **Where might be the best place to interrupt this cycle?**

....

....

....

....

REFLECTION QUESTIONS _____

1. Which component of the Blame Loop resonates most strongly with your experience?

....

....

....

2. What patterns do you notice playing out across different areas of your life?

....

....

....

3. When have you successfully broken free from a Blame Loop in the past?

_____

_____

_____

4. What could become possible if you removed the keystone of Blind Blaming?

_____

_____

_____

COMMITMENT TO BREAKING THE LOOP

Based on what you've discovered in this chapter, identify one specific action to begin breaking your Blame Loop:

- **The component I will focus on disrupting is:**

_____

- **The specific action I will take is:**

_____

- **I will know this is working when:**

_____

- **The support I need to maintain this change is:**

_____

JOURNAL PROMPT: Before moving to the next section, reflect on what it feels like to recognize your Blame Loop. What emotions arise as you see these patterns? What resistance do you notice? What new possibilities are emerging as you consider breaking free?

Understanding the Blame Loop isn't just about recognizing patterns; it's about finding the fault lines in our psychological bedrock where transformation becomes possible. Real breakthroughs don't come from adding more layers to our existing paradigms but from pressure applied at the right points, in the right ways.

Turn the page to begin Section Two: The RCD Method™, where we'll learn a powerful three-step process for breaking free from the Blame Loop.

SECTION TWO

THE RCD METHOD™

THE RCD METHOD ™

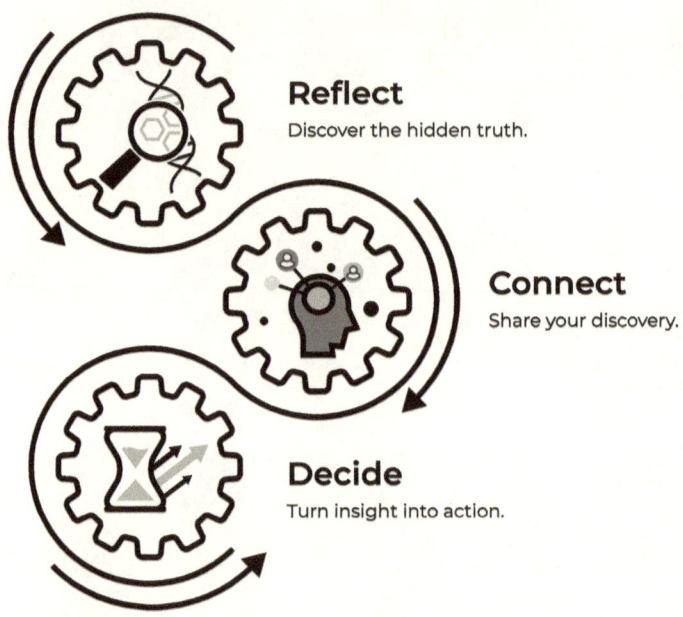

Reflect
Discover the hidden truth.

Connect
Share your discovery.

Decide
Turn insight into action.

Obstacle Deep Nexus Analysis (O-DNA)

When you'are **HEALTHY** and clear on your **PURPOSE**, committed to **GROWTH**, supported by strong **RELATIONSHIPS**, and equipped with the right **RESOURCES**, you can overcome any obstacle.

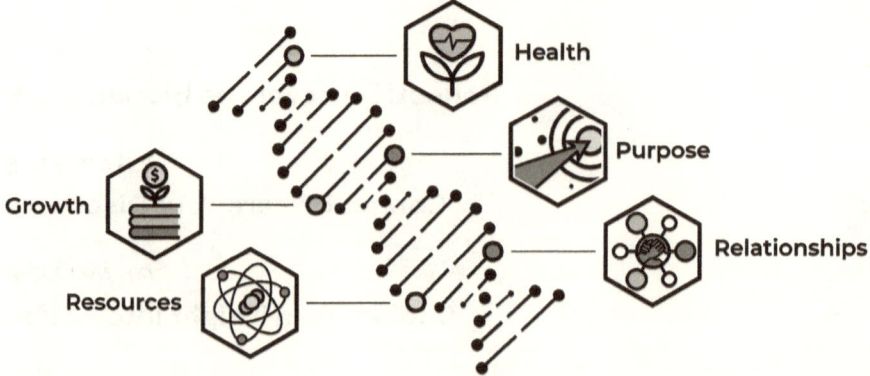

Health

Purpose

Growth

Relationships

Resources

Chapter 4

REFLECT: DISCOVER THE HIDDEN TRUTH

WHEN SOMETHING IS HOLDING YOU BACK, the real obstacle often isn't what you think it is. Traditional problem-solving approaches fail us time and time again because we get caught in the Blame Loop, pointing fingers at surface-level issues while the real cause remains hidden.

THE RCD METHOD: A NEW APPROACH

Definition: The RCD Method™ is a three-step process for uncovering and overcoming what's really holding you back:

1. **Reflect:** Discover the hidden truth using O-DNA analysis

2. **Connect:** Share your discovery with outside perspective

3. **Decide:** Turn insight into action

Instead of asking, "What is the problem?" or "Who is to blame?" the RCD Method starts with a more powerful question: **"Is there something else going on?"**

 **REMEMBER THIS:** This shift—from looking for problems to discovering hidden truths—changes everything.

CONNECTING TO YOUR STORY

Look back at your blind blaming story and identify the moment of reflection that led to your breakthrough:

■ **What question or insight helped you see beyond the surface problem?**

....

....

....

....

■ **Who or what provided the perspective that helped you see differently?**

....

....

....

....

■ **What became clear once you discovered the hidden truth?**

....

....

....

....

OBSTACLES VS. PROBLEMS: WORDS MATTER

When we label our challenges as "problems," we often see them as permanent conditions to be endured. When we reframe them as "obstacles," we recognize them as something to be navigated, crossed, or transformed.

■ **Choose a current challenge and reframe it:**

As a problem:

....

As an obstacle:

....

■ **How does this shift in language change how you feel about the situation?**

....

....

....

■ **How does it change what actions seem possible?**

....

....

....

THE POWER OF O-DNA:
YOUR DISCOVERY FRAMEWORK

O-DNA (Obstacle Deep Nexus Analysis) examines five core areas, or "strands," where your root cause might be hiding:

1. **Health:** Your foundation for everything

2. **Purpose:** Your inner compass

3. **Relationships:** Your connections

4. **Growth:** Your evolution engine

5. **Resources:** Your support system

The key is understanding that you're not trying to fix all five areas. You're using them as lenses to find that ONE thing that has been hiding in plain sight—the real root cause that, once addressed, will create a ripple effect of positive change.

O-DNA ANALYSIS: MAPPING YOUR OBSTACLE

Think about a significant obstacle you're currently facing. For each strand, answer the questions honestly and look for patterns:

THE HEALTH STRAND

■ **Rate yourself (1–5) on each aspect of the Health Strand:**

○ **Physical Activity:** Daily movement of at least 45 minutes

○ **Medical Oversight:** Regular preventive checkups

○ **Hormone Health:** Regular hormone monitoring

○ **Nutrition Strategy:** Structured approach to fueling your body

○ **Sleep Quality:** 7-8 hours of quality sleep nightly

■ **What patterns do you notice in your health that might be affecting this obstacle?**

....

....

....

....

■ **What symptoms have you been normalizing or attributing to stress?**

....

....

....

....

THE PURPOSE STRAND

■ **Rate yourself (1–5) on each aspect of the Purpose Strand:**

◯ **Mission Clarity:** Clear written personal mission statement

◯ **Purpose Definition:** Core purpose articulated in one sentence

◯ **Values Integration:** Nonnegotiable values with clarifying statements

◯ **Achievement Focus:** Clear high-impact goal identified

◯ **Daily Priorities:** First three hours align with purpose

■ **Where do you see disconnects between your stated mission and daily actions?**

....

....

....

....

■ **Which decisions feel difficult despite having clear purpose and values?**

....

....

....

....

THE RELATIONSHIPS STRAND

■ **Rate yourself (1–5) on each aspect of the Relationships Strand:**

◯ **Clear Communication:** Expressing needs and expectations

◯ **Feedback Openness:** Inviting and accepting honest input

◯ **Healthy Boundaries:** Protecting your energy

◯ **Deep Connections:** Having real, honest relationships

◯ **Conflict Resolution:** Addressing issues directly

■ **What patterns do you notice in how you respond to emotional situations?**

....

....

....

....

■ **Which relationships consistently drain or energize you, and why?**

....

....

....

....

THE GROWTH STRAND

■ **Rate yourself (1-5) on each aspect of the Growth Strand:**

◯ **Learning Commitment:** Daily deliberate reading, watching or listening

◯ Challenge Response: Embracing unfamiliar situations

◯ Failure Perspective: Extracting lessons from setbacks

◯ Skill Development: Actively developing new abilities

◯ Growth Environment: Surrounding yourself with challenge

- **Where do you consistently avoid challenges or stay in your comfort zone?**

....

....

....

....

- **What skills have you convinced yourself you "can't learn"?**

....

....

....

....

THE RESOURCES STRAND

- **Rate yourself (1–5) on each aspect of the Resources Strand:**

◯ **Strategic Planning:** System for planning and execution

◯ **Feedback & Measurement:** Clear indicators of progress

◯ **Decision Optimization:** Frameworks for analysis

◯ **Accountability Systems:** External structures for follow-through

◯ **Environmental Design:** Surroundings support success

■ **What systems have you been avoiding but know would help?**

....

....

....

....

■ **How is your environment either supporting or sabotaging your goals?**

....

....

....

....

FINDING YOUR HIDDEN TRUTH

Review your responses across all five strands. Look for connections, patterns, and potential root causes.

■ **What strand scored lowest overall?**

....

....

....

....

■ **What connections do you notice between different strands?**

....

....

....

■ **What made you defensive or uncomfortable during this analysis?**

....

....

....

■ **Based on this analysis, what ONE thing, once addressed, could create positive change across ALL areas?**

....

....

....

■ **Why might this have been difficult to see before now?**

....

....

....

REFLECTION QUESTIONS _____

1. Which O-DNA strand revealed the most surprising insights?

_____

_____

_____

2. What patterns emerged across different areas of your life?

_____

_____

_____

3. What "reasonable explanations" might be masking deeper truths?

_____

_____

_____

4. What ONE change could positively impact all five O-DNA strands?

_____

_____

_____

Based on what you've discovered through O-DNA analysis, commit to one specific action:

■ **The hidden truth I've discovered is:**

....

■ **The one action I'll take to address this root cause is:**

....

■ **I'll take this action by (date/time):**

....

■ **I'll know this is working when:**

....

JOURNAL PROMPT: Before moving to the next chapter, write freely about what you've discovered through O-DNA analysis. What surprises you most? What confirms what you've suspected? What feels most important to address? What questions remain?

....

....

....

....

_____

_____

_____

_____

_____

_____

_____

_____

_____

_____

Finding your root cause through O-DNA is powerful, but it's only the first step. Our blind spots exist for a reason—they often protect us from uncomfortable truths or challenging changes. That's why the next chapter is crucial. We'll explore how to take your discovery outside your sphere of influence, connecting with others who can help validate your findings and strengthen your resolve for change.

Turn the page to explore Chapter 5, where we'll learn how to share our discoveries with those who can help us see more clearly.

THE RCD METHOD ™

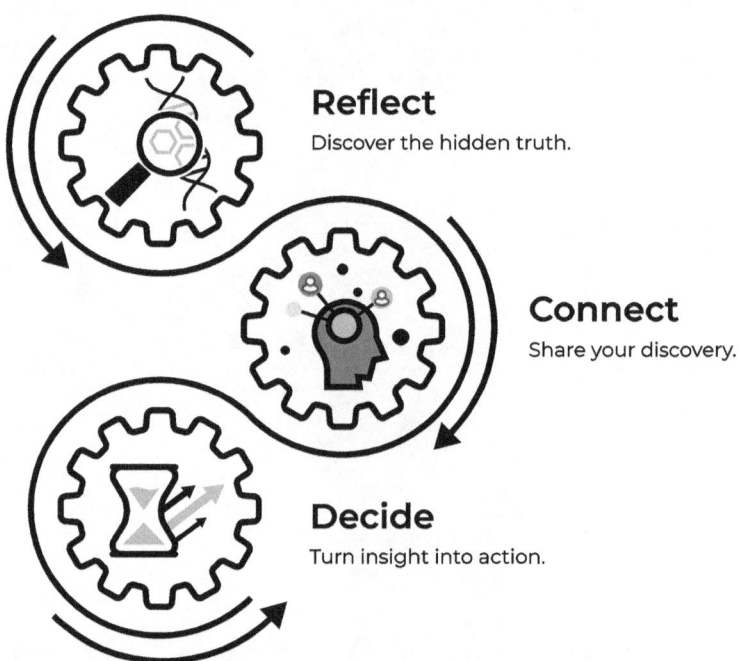

Reflect
Discover the hidden truth.

Connect
Share your discovery.

Decide
Turn insight into action.

Chapter 5

CONNECT: SHARE YOUR DISCOVERY

WHEN SURGEONS FACE THEIR MOST challenging cases, they don't just consult with colleagues down the hall. They reach out to specialists at other hospitals, present at international conferences, and seek insights from experts across the globe. Yet in business and personal life, we often try to solve our biggest challenges on our own or by consulting only those within our sphere of influence—the very people who share our blind spots.

THE POWER OF OUTSIDE PERSPECTIVE

Definition: The Connect stage is about breaking free from the Blame Loop by seeking wisdom from outside your sphere of influence—from people who are not caught in the same thought patterns or bound by the same assumptions.

This is crucial because the people closest to your situation—your team, family, friends, or advisors—are often caught in the same patterns of Blind Blaming that you are.

 **REMEMBER THIS:** If everyone in your current sphere could see the root cause of your obstacle, wouldn't they have pointed it out already?

CONNECTING TO YOUR STORY

Look back at your blind blaming story and identify how outside perspective played a role:

■ **Who provided the perspective that helped you see differently?**

....

....

....

....

■ **Why were they able to see what others (including you) missed?**

....

....

....

....

■ **How did their perspective change your understanding?**

....

....

....

....

THE TWO FORCES OF CONNECTION

The Connect stage relies on two distinct forces that must come from outside your regular sphere of influence:

1. The Catalyst: Your Professional Coach

A catalyst creates the conditions for breakthroughs without solving your problems for you. Because they are outside your sphere of influence, they can:

- See patterns that everyone inside your sphere has normalized
- Ask questions that those close to you won't ask
- Challenge assumptions that your regular circle shares
- Push past the comfortable explanations everyone has accepted

2. The Collective: Your Mastermind Group

A collective combines the power of multiple perspectives from people not caught in your current situation. Because they are outside your sphere of influence, they can:

- Spot patterns that your current circle has become blind to
- Share solutions that worked in similar but different contexts
- Challenge your thinking without personal agenda
- Provide feedback untainted by office politics or family dynamics

Why do both forces matter? One sparks the breakthrough; the other helps ensure it sticks.

MAPPING YOUR CURRENT SPHERE OF INFLUENCE

Before seeking outside perspective, it's important to understand who's currently influencing your thinking:

■ **List the 5-7 people you typically turn to for advice or perspective:**

1. .... Relationship: ....

2. .... Relationship: ....

3. .... Relationship: ....

4. .... Relationship: ....

5. .... Relationship: ....

6. .... Relationship: ....

7. .... Relationship: ....

■ **What shared blind spots might exist within this group?**

....

....

....

....

■ **What perspectives are missing from this circle?**

....

....

....

....

FINDING YOUR CATALYST

A professional coach serves as a catalyst for your personal insights and growth. The right coach:

- Asks powerful questions rather than giving answers
- Illuminates blind spots without judgment
- Maintains unwavering accountability
- Guides you through proven frameworks
- Challenges limiting assumptions and beliefs

Based on your O-DNA analysis, what type of coach might best serve your needs?

....

....

....

What specific expertise or experience should they have?

....

....

....

What qualities would make them an effective catalyst for you personally?

....

....

....

FINDING YOUR COLLECTIVE

While coaching provides individualized guidance, mastermind groups offer the power of collective wisdom. The right mastermind:

- Meets regularly with structured agendas
- Includes members at or above your level
- Represents diverse experiences but similar ambitions
- Maintains strict confidentiality
- Holds each other accountable for growth

What type of mastermind group would complement your growth needs?

....

....

....

What perspectives would be most valuable in this collective?

....

....

....

How would you contribute to such a group?

....

....

....

PREPARING TO SHARE YOUR DISCOVERY

The quality of the insights you receive depends on how you prepare to share your O-DNA discoveries:

■ **Summarize your O-DNA findings in 2-3 clear sentences:**

....

....

....

....

■ **What specific questions do you have about these findings?**

....

....

....

....

■ **What patterns are you still uncertain about?**

....

....

....

....

■ **What resistance might you need help overcoming?**

....

....

....

....

THE INVESTMENT QUESTION

"How much does it cost?" is often the first question people ask about coaching and mastermind groups. But let's reframe this question: What is the cost of staying stuck?

Calculate your "stuck cost":

Current annual cost of this obstacle (time/money/energy): $............................

Projected 5-year cost if unresolved: $............................

Potential value of a breakthrough solution: $............................

Opportunity cost of delayed transformation: $............................

■ **Looking at these numbers, what would be a reasonable investment in the right guidance?**

....

....

....

....

■ **What beliefs do you hold about investing in your own growth?**

....

....

....

....

MAXIMIZING YOUR CONNECTIONS

Finding the right connections is only the first step. Making them work requires commitment:

For working with a coach, I commit to:

☐ Scheduling sessions before anything else on my calendar

☐ Spending at least 30 minutes preparing for each session

☐ Reviewing my O-DNA insights regularly

☐ Being distraction-free during sessions

☐ Implementing insights and actions discussed

☐ Taking full responsibility for my growth journey

For engaging with a mastermind group, I commit to:

☐ Attending and participating fully in every session

☐ Preparing thoroughly for each meeting

☐ Sharing my true challenges, not just my successes

☐ Acting on the insights I receive

☐ Contributing generously to others' growth

☐ Honoring my commitment to the group

REFLECTION QUESTIONS

1. What resistance do you notice to seeking outside perspective?

....

....

....

....

2. What blind spots might your current advisors share with you?

....

....

....

....

3. What would becoming "unstuck" be worth to you?

....

....

....

4. How ready are you to be challenged by perspectives that might contradict your current understanding?

....

....

....

COMMITMENT TO CONNECTION

Based on what you've discovered in this chapter, commit to one specific action to expand your sphere of influence:

■ **The connection I will seek is:**

....

■ **My first step toward this connection will be:**

....

■ **I will take this step by (date):**

....

■ **The support I need to follow through is:**

....

JOURNAL PROMPT: Before moving to the next chapter, reflect on your feelings about seeking outside perspective. What excites you? What scares you? What hopes do you have for what others might see that you cannot? What fears do you have about what they might discover?

....

....

....

_____

_____

_____

_____

_____

_____

_____

_____

_____

_____

_____

The right connections can transform how you see yourself and your challenges. By seeking perspectives outside your sphere of influence, you create the conditions for breakthroughs that would be impossible on your own. This isn't about admitting defeat—it's about acknowledging that we all have blind spots, and that true growth often comes from allowing others to illuminate what we cannot see.

Turn the page to explore Chapter 6, where we'll learn how to turn insights into decisive action.

Chapter 6

DECIDE: TURN INSIGHT INTO ACTION

THE LAST STAGE OF THE TRANSFORMATIVE RCD Method is Decide, which deals with the power of decision-making. You've done the reflection. You've got an outside perspective. Now it's time to Make a Fucking Decision (MFD) and move forward.

THE POWER OF DECISIVE ACTION

Definition: Making a Fucking Decision (MFD) means more than just choosing. It means breaking free from the paralysis that keeps you stuck. While others are still analyzing, debating, and seeking consensus, successful people are taking action and learning from the results.

When you Make a Fucking Decision, you step into your power as a decision-maker—no more hiding behind analysis paralysis, waiting for perfect certainty, trying to please everyone, or using "what-ifs" as an excuse for inaction.

 **REMEMBER THIS:** A good decision executed with complete conviction will almost always outperform a perfect decision executed with hesitation—or worse, never executed at all.

CONNECTING TO YOUR STORY

Look back at your blind blaming story and identify the decision that changed everything:

■ **What decision did you finally make that created breakthrough?**

....

....

....

....

■ **What made this decision different from previous attempts?**

....

....

....

....

■ **How did making this decision affect your energy and outlook?**

....

....

....

....

....

WHY DECISIONS GET STUCK

Here is the pathway that well-intentioned people go down when they experience decision-making paralysis:

- You see the real problem clearly through O-DNA (Reflect).
- You get valuable outside perspective (Connect).
- Then, you hesitate. You analyze. You wait.
- And nothing changes.

■ **Which of these decision blockers do you recognize in yourself? Check all that apply:**

☐ **Analysis Paralysis:** Endless research and comparison

☐ **Perfectionism:** Waiting for the "perfect" solution

☐ **People Pleasing:** Trying to make everyone happy

☐ **Fear of Failure:** Worrying about making the wrong choice

☐ **Fear of Success:** Unconscious resistance to growth

☐ **Competing Priorities:** Unable to choose what matters most

☐ **Overwhelm:** Too many options causing shutdown

☐ **Indecisiveness Habit:** Pattern of deferring decisions

■ **For the blockers you checked, describe how they typically show up for you:**

....

....

....

....

MAKING YOUR FUCKING DECISION

The path to your MFD begins with four essential questions:

1. What is the real problem? Not the surface issue, but the truth your O-DNA revealed and your connections confirmed:

....

....

....

2. What is the clear path forward? Not the perfect answer, but a direction that aligns with your reflection and outside perspective:

....

....

....

3. What is really stopping me? Be brutally honest about what's holding you back:

....

....

....

4. When will I decide? Set a specific date and time:

....

....

....

THE BEAUTIFUL SIMPLICITY OF DECISION

The formula for making your fucking decision is beautifully simple:

1. Name the real problem.

2. Choose your path.

3. Fucking commit to it.

■ **Draft your decision statement below:**

I am deciding to ....

instead of ....

starting ....

because ....

This will create ....

I commit fully by ....

MAKING IT STICK

Once you've made your fucking decision, three critical elements will determine its success:

1. Immediate Action What action will you take within one minute of your decision?

....

....

....

What visible momentum will you create in the first 24 hours?

....

....

....

2. Clear Communication Who needs to know about your decision?

....

....

....

How will you communicate it with clarity and conviction?

....

....

....

3. Unwavering Focus How will you keep your decision front and center daily?

....

....

....

What metrics will you track to measure progress?

....

....

....

YOUR IMPLEMENTATION TIMELINE

A decision without implementation is just a thought. Create your action plan:

First 60 Seconds:

- ■ ....

- ■ ....

First 24 Hours:

- ■ ....

- ■ ....

First Week:

- ■ ....

- ■ ....

First Month:

- ■ ....

- ■ ....

First Quarter:

- ■ ....

- ■ ....

■ What early wins will you celebrate?

■ How will you handle inevitable obstacles?

REFLECTION QUESTIONS

1. What decision have you been avoiding that's keeping you stuck?

2. What is the real cost of not deciding?

3. What becomes possible once you decide?

....

....

....

4. What is the worst that could happen if you commit?

....

....

....

COMMITMENT TO DECISION

This is your moment of truth—the point where insight transforms into action:

▪ **My Fucking Decision is:**

....

▪ **I am fully committing to this because:**

....

▪ **I will begin implementation on (exact date/time):**

....

■ **My first three actions will be:**

....

I'm signing my name as a commitment to this decision:

Signature: .... Date: ....

JOURNAL PROMPT: Before moving to the next section, write about how it feels to make your fucking decision. What shifts in your energy do you notice? What fears arise? What excitement builds? What feels different now compared to before you decided?

....

....

....

....

....

....

....

....

CASE STUDY REFLECTION:
WHEN MARKETING ISN'T THE PROBLEM

Christina's tech company was losing market share despite tripling their marketing budget. She blamed marketing messages until she asked, "What if marketing isn't the problem?" Her O-DNA revealed they had stopped evolving their product while the market transformed.

■ **Reflection: Where might you be focusing on the wrong solution like Christina did?**

....

....

....

....

■ **How could asking "What if [your current explanation] isn't the problem?" shift your perspective?**

....

....

....

....

CASE STUDY REFLECTION: BEYOND "JUST TALK IT OUT"

Amelia and David's marriage was falling apart despite multiple therapists. They blamed communication until medical tests revealed David's low testosterone and Amelia's anxiety were creating a perfect storm of misunderstanding.

■ **Reflection: Where might health factors be influencing a challenge you've attributed to something else?**

....

....

....

....

■ **What physical aspects of your situation might deserve attention?**

....

....

....

....

....

CASE STUDY REFLECTION: WHEN INTENSITY ISN'T THE ANSWER

Carrie spent years and thousands on intense workouts with minimal results. She blamed her effort level until discovering her focus on high-intensity training had led to neglecting basic movement patterns.

■ **Reflection: Where might you be pushing harder when a different approach is needed?**

....

....

....

....

....

■ **What might "less intense but more effective" look like in your situation?**

....

....

....

....

....

CASE STUDY REFLECTION:
WHEN LOYALTY ISN'T THE ISSUE

Tom's tech company was losing talented employees despite rapid growth. He blamed generational attitudes until O-DNA revealed their "loyalty problem" was actually a growth obstacle—they'd invested in expansion but neglected development.

■ **Reflection: Where might you be misinterpreting others' behaviors or motivations?**

....

....

....

....

■ **What investment in development might solve a seemingly unrelated problem?**

....

....

....

....

CASE STUDY REFLECTION:
WHEN CONFIDENCE ISN'T THE ANSWER

Kim's career stalled despite her brilliance. She blamed her confidence and sought perfection until discovering her perfectionism was a barrier to authentic connection—with others and herself.

Reflection: Where might perfectionism be blocking your progress?

....

....

....

....

....

How might authenticity create breakthroughs where performance has failed?

....

....

....

....

....

CASE STUDY REFLECTION:
WHEN MAKING MORE ISN'T THE ANSWER

Anthony struggled financially despite his six-figure income. He blamed his earnings until O-DNA revealed his money problem was actually a purpose obstacle—his financial decisions weren't aligned with his true values.

■ **Reflection: Where might alignment with values matter more than additional resources?**

....

....

....

....

....

■ **What purpose misalignment might be creating challenges in your situation?**

....

....

....

....

CASE STUDY REFLECTION: WHEN TRADITION ISN'T THE ANSWER

Michael's film studio faced declining box office returns. He blamed streaming services until he realized their resistance to change wasn't protecting the business—it was preventing evolution.

- **Reflection: Where might resistance to change be disguised as principle or tradition in your life?**

....

....

....

....

- **What evolution might you be resisting that could create breakthrough?**

....

....

....

....

CREATING YOUR CASE STUDY

Now it's time to craft your own case study—the story of your breakthrough journey:

- **Initial Situation:** Describe your starting point and the challenge you faced:

....

....

....

....

- **Negativity to Possibility:** How did you shift from blame to curiosity?

....

....

....

....

- **Breaking Free from the Blame Loop:** What patterns did you recognize once you stopped blaming?

....

....

....

....

- **Application of the RCD Method:** How did you Reflect, Connect, and Decide?

  ....

  ....

  ....

  ....

- **Results:** What transformation have you experienced or do you anticipate?

  ....

  ....

  ....

  ....

- **Key Insights:** What fundamental truth did you discover?

  ....

  ....

  ....

  ....

YOUR TRANSFORMATION LEGACY

Your breakthrough journey isn't just for you—it has the potential to help others:

■ **Who else might benefit from hearing your story?**

....

....

....

....

■ **What aspect of your journey might be most helpful to others?**

....

....

....

....

■ **How might you share your insights with those who need them?**

....

....

....

....

REFLECTION QUESTIONS

1. What patterns do you notice across all seven case studies?

   ....

   ....

   ....

   ....

2. Which transformation resonated most deeply with you and why?

   ....

   ....

   ....

   ....

3. What stage of transformation do you believe you're currently in?

   ....

   ....

   ....

   ....

4. What feels most important to remember from these stories?

   ....

   ....

   ....

COMMITMENT TO TRANSFORMATION

Based on the insights from these case studies and your own journey:

■ **The transformation I am committed to creating is:**

....

....

■ **I will know I'm successful when:**

....

....

■ **The support I need to maintain this transformation is:**

....

....

■ **The first person I will share my journey with is:**

....

....

JOURNAL PROMPT: Before moving to the conclusion, reflect on your entire journey through this journal. What has shifted in how you see your challenges? What new possibilities have emerged? What feels different about how you approach obstacles now? What are you most grateful for discovering?

....

....

....

....

These seven stories illustrate a fundamental truth about meaningful change: Breakthroughs happen when we shift from surface-level solutions to systemic understanding. Through the RCD Method—Reflect, Connect, Decide—these individuals not only solved problems, they transformed their entire approach to obstacles, creating ripple effects that extended far beyond their initial challenges.

Turn the page for the conclusion of your breakthrough journey, where we'll reflect on your path forward beyond blind blaming.

Conclusion

YOUR PATH FORWARD

STILL KEEP THAT OLD, SCUFFED BASEBALL on my desk. Its worn leather tells a story—my story—of standing awkwardly on a dusty field, unable to see what everyone else took for granted. That baseball reminds me daily that our most significant breakthroughs often come not from trying harder but from seeing clearer.

Your journey through this journal has been about turning on the lights and seeing what's been hiding in plain sight. It's been about discovering that you are not failing at solving your problems—you are succeeding perfectly at solving the wrong ones.

YOUR JOURNEY IN REVIEW

Take a moment to reflect on your breakthrough journey:

- **From Chapter 1: Understanding Blind Blaming** What key insight did you gain about your blind blaming patterns?

....

....

....

....

■ **From Chapter 2: Negativity to Possibility** How has your relationship to blaming and complaining shifted?

....

....

....

....

■ **From Chapter 3: The Blame Loop Revealed** Which component of the Blame Loop had the strongest hold on you?

....

....

....

....

■ **From Chapter 4: Reflect: Discover the Hidden Truth** What hidden truth did O–DNA analysis reveal?

....

....

....

....

From Chapter 5: Connect: Share Your Discovery How did outside perspective change your understanding?

....

....

....

....

From Chapter 6: Decide: Turn Insight into Action What decision transformed possibility into reality?

....

....

....

....

From Chapter 7: Real-World Examples Which case study provided the most valuable insight?

....

....

....

....

THE HIDDEN TRUTH REVEALED

Our journey revealed three crucial strategies that transform how we approach challenges:

1. Moving from Negativity to Possibility How has stopping blame and complaint created space for new perspectives?

....

....

....

....

2. Breaking Free from the Blame Loop How has recognizing your patterns allowed you to see your situation clearly?

....

....

....

....

3. Using the RCD Method How has Reflect, Connect, and Decide created lasting change?

....

....

....

....

WRITING YOUR NEW STORY

Your breakthrough journey has changed your narrative. Take a moment to write your story—not as it was, but as it is now:

■ Beginning: Where I was

_____

_____

_____

■ Middle: What I discovered

_____

_____

_____

■ New Chapter: Where I'm headed

_____

_____

_____

_____

YOUR TRANSFORMATION TOOLKIT

As you continue beyond this journal, remember these essential tools:

1. **O-DNA Analysis** When facing obstacles, examine all five strands:

   - Health: Your physical and mental well-being patterns
   - Purpose: Your mission and values alignment
   - Relationships: Your connection and support networks
   - Growth: Your learning and development edges
   - Resources: Your time, energy, and asset flows

2. **Strategic Connection** Continuously seek perspectives outside your sphere:

   - Professional coaching for catalytic insights
   - Mastermind groups for collective wisdom
   - Diverse viewpoints to challenge assumptions

3. **Decisive Action** Transform possibility into reality through:

   - Clear decisions without hedging
   - Immediate implementation
   - Consistent follow-through

- **Which tool will be most important in your continued journey?**

THE FINAL TRUTH

Your obstacles are not random. They have specific DNA unique to you, which you can understand through reflection and self-awareness. These challenges are not just there to trip you up; they hold lessons and insights that, once uncovered, can help you move forward.

Your blind spots, the areas you can't see on your own, become visible through connection—with others, mentors, and people who can offer a different perspective.

Your breakthrough, the moment everything changes, happens when you finally Make a Fucking Decision to act. Not when you're stuck over-thinking or waiting for the "right time," but when you act with clarity and courage.

■ **What is the most important truth you've discovered on this journey?**

YOUR ONGOING COMMITMENT

Your breakthrough journey doesn't end with the closing of this journal. It continues with your daily choices and actions.

■ **I commit to continuing my breakthrough journey by:**

....

....

....

....

....

....

....

....

....

....

....

....

....

When I notice blind blaming patterns returning, I will:

_____

_____

_____

_____

_____

_____

I will share what I've learned with others by:

_____

_____

_____

_____

_____

_____

_____

DRAFT A LETTER FROM YOUR FUTURE SELF

A Guided Exercise to Break Free from the
Blame Loop and Gain Clarity

INTRODUCTION: WHY WRITE A LETTER FROM YOUR FUTURE SELF?

Most people are stuck solving the wrong problems because they are trapped in **Blind Blaming**—blaming circumstances, other people, or even themselves without uncovering the real root cause. Writing a letter from your **future self** is a powerful tool to help break free from the **Blame Loop** by shifting perspective, setting clear intentions, and visualizing the path forward.

Your future self has already **broken the loop** and can now guide you with wisdom, confidence, and clarity.

STEP-BY-STEP INSTRUCTIONS

1. Set the Timeframe

- Choose a point in the future:
  - **1 year from now** (short-term transformation)
  - **5 years from now** (long-term vision)
  - **10+ years from now** (legacy thinking)
- Your future self is writing to you today, sharing insights on how you overcame your struggles and solved the **real** problem.

2. Reflect on Where You Are Now

Before your future self can guide you, acknowledge where you are:

- What challenges are you currently facing?
- What are you blaming others (or yourself) for?
- What areas of life feel **stuck** (health, relationships, wealth, career)?
- What decisions have you been avoiding?

Write a few sentences about your current situation before moving on.

....

....

....

....

....

3. Step into Your Future Self's Mindset

Imagine your **future self** has already broken free from **Blind Blaming** and solved the **root cause** of today's problems. From that perspective, write a letter to your present self answering these key questions:

- **What breakthrough did I have that changed everything?**
- **What false assumptions did I let go of?** (Hint: These may come from Preconceived Perceptions or Receptive Rigidity in the Blame Loop.)
- **What new habits, mindsets, or decisions led to real transformation?**
- **What advice do I have for my past self who still feels stuck?**

4. Make It Personal and Encouraging

- Use a **warm, direct tone**, like an older, wiser mentor version of yourself.

- Include **specific moments**—what you learned, when it "clicked," and how you took action.

- Acknowledge that the **struggle was real**, but **the solution was within reach.**

- Offer **forgiveness** for past mistakes and **encouragement** to move forward.

Example Opening:

"Hey [Your Name], I know you're frustrated right now. I remember exactly how it felt to be stuck in that endless loop, thinking you had a clear problem but actually chasing the wrong one. I wish I could reach back and show you the truth sooner, but you had to go through it to get here. The moment everything changed was when you finally..."

5. Commit to Action

Your future self has **already taken action** to break the Blame Loop. End the letter with:

- **A clear message to your present self** about the **first step** to take today.

- A reminder that **real transformation** happens when you take ownership.

- Encouragement to trust the process, even when it's uncomfortable.

Example Closing:

"You don't need to have all the answers today. Just take the first step—ask a better question, challenge an old belief, or take that action you've been avoiding. I promise, the life you're meant for is waiting on the other side. See you soon."

6. Read It Back and Internalize It

- Read your letter out loud.

- Notice any **emotional reactions**—relief, excitement, resistance.

- Underline key insights that **surprise you** (this might reveal what's really holding you back).

- Keep it somewhere you can revisit when doubt creeps in.

■ **Take a moment to write a letter to your future self—the one who might be tempted to return to old patterns of blind blaming. What would you want to remind yourself?**

Dear ....,

....

....

....

....

....

....

....

CONNECTING TO YOUR STORY

As you read these case studies, notice which elements resonate with your own experience:

■ **Which case study feels most similar to your situation? Why?**

....

....

....

■ **What patterns do you recognize from your own journey?**

....

....

....

■ **What hope do these stories give you for your own transformation?**

....

....

....

Chapter 7

REAL-WORLD EXAMPLES

EVERY BREAKTHROUGH JOURNEY IS UNIQUE, yet patterns of transformation repeat across different lives and situations. This chapter invites you to explore seven transformative stories and connect them to your own experience. These real-world examples will help you see that your challenges are not random—they follow recognizable patterns that, once understood, become signposts pointing toward your own transformation. Be sure to have the book, Beyond Blame Blaming for this exercise so you can reference the case studies in the book.

THE POWER OF OTHERS' STORIES

Definition: Case studies aren't just interesting stories—they're maps of possibility. By studying how others moved beyond blind blaming, you can discover patterns applicable to your own situation. Each case study reveals how someone:

- Moved from Negativity to Possibility
- Broke Free from the Blame Loop
- Applied the RCD Method
- Created lasting Results

 **REMEMBER THIS:** The most valuable insights often come from seeing your patterns reflected in someone else's journey.

SECTION THREE

TRANSFORMATION

The RCD Method ensures that when you reach the decision point, you can act with clear vision (Reflect), valuable perspective (Connect), and committed action (Decide). A decision without action is just a thought. A decision without communication is just a secret. A decision without focus is just a moment. But a decision with all three elements becomes unstoppable.

Turn the page to begin Section Three: Transformation, where we'll explore real-world examples of people who have moved beyond blind blaming.

_____

_____

_____

_____

_____

_____

_____

_____

_____

_____

_____

_____

_____

_____

With clarity and courage,

[Your name] _____

Date: _____

FINAL JOURNAL PROMPT: As you complete this journal, reflect on your entire journey. What has been your most profound discovery? What feels different now? What possibilities have opened that weren't visible before? What are you most grateful for learning?

_____

_____

_____

_____

_____

_____

_____

_____

_____

_____

REMEMBER: Life is too short to stay trapped in patterns that no longer serve you. Don't let Blind Blaming keep you from seeing the true nature of your obstacles. Your breakthrough journey starts with seeing clearly, connecting authentically, and deciding bravely.

Your journey beyond Blind Blaming continues with each choice, each day, each step forward.

Make your fucking decision. Take action. Your breakthrough awaits.

Want more information or help?

VISIT

www.BlindBlaming.com